The Sporting News PRESENTS

Game Faces

A COLLECTION OF OUR GREATEST BASEBALL PORTRAITS

ACKNOWLEDGEMENTS

If a picture is worth a thousand words, the words of thanks here will come nowhere close to expressing the depth of passion that accompanies each and every photograph in this book ...

It must start, however, with the men and women whose photographs compose The Sporting News collection. Without their work, whether it be 1903 or 1993, this book would not be possible. Today, a staff of phenomenally talented photographers—Albert Dickson, Bob Leverone, Robert Seale and Dilip Vishwanat—shoot for The Sporting News. Many thousands of thank yous to each of you. And thanks to Fred Barnes and Paul Nisely, who guide and edit the photo staff day-to-day, week-to-week.

Choosing the best images and creating an effective design were the daunting tasks faced by Bob Parajon with the help of Michael Behrens and Christen Sager, who spent countless hours collecting, editing and organizing hundreds of images. But as you'll see, this was far from a 'task' for them; it was an opportunity to showcase their talent and passion to the project, and it shows.

Making sure each image reproduced in print as brilliantly as it was captured on film was the job of prepress specialist Steve Romer, whose meticulous scanning, color correction and retouching is evident in every photograph.

Thanks to the staff of The Sporting News Research Center—Steve Gietschier, Jim Meier and Bob Mayhall—who maintain the collection of images and know just where to find things. And thanks to Joe Hoppel, who provided a valuable assist in organizing this book.

Steve Meyerhoff
Editorial Director, Books Publishing Division

Game Faces

CONTENTS

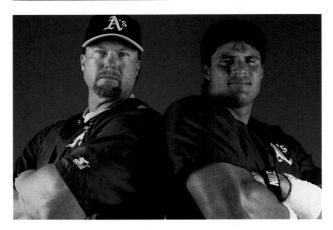

110 ACES

138 SLUGGERS

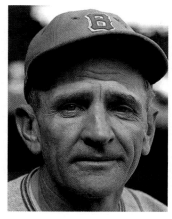

180 SKIPPERS & THE BOSS

198 EXTRA INNINGS

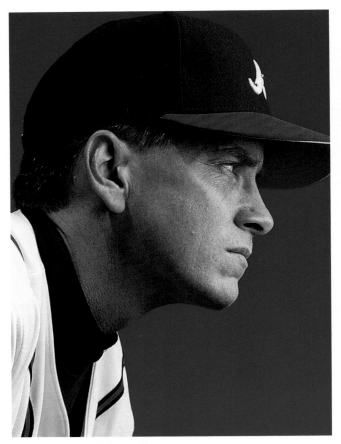

TOM GLAVINE, 2000

TY COBB, 1927

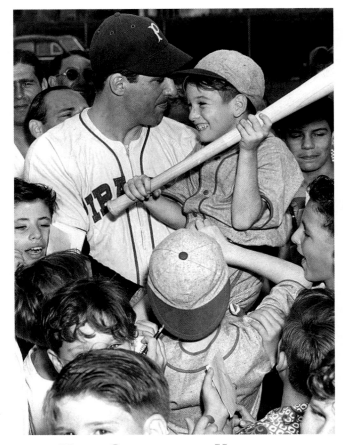

HANK GREENBERG & KIDS, 1947

MARK MCGWIRE & KIDS, 1997

INTRODUCTION

The history of The Sporting News dates back more than a century, to 1886. In that March 17, 1886, issue, the front page featured articles headlined:

The Game in Gotham

Harry Wright's Team
He Says the Phillies Will Be Among the Leaders This Year

The White Stockings
Chicago's Great Team Getting Ready for the Trip to Hot Springs

Though baseball wasn't in the organized form it is today—that came in 1901, when the American League was created and ushered in The Modern Era—baseball still was at the very core of that very first issue of the weekly newspaper.

Line-drawings were used to illustrate the publication in its early years. It wasn't until 1902 that photographs made their debut in the publication. That first picture: pitcher Charles W. Harper.

Thus was born the combination that comes together in the subsequent pages of this book. And it's a powerful combination. The Sporting News maintains an ever-growing collection of baseball images that numbers in the hundreds of thousands, from Babe Ruth to Mark McGwire. From Lou Gehrig to Cal Ripken. From Stan Musial to Tony Gwynn.

We've compiled some of the best of those pictures. Get ready to look into the eyes and into the very soul of baseball history.

KERRY WOOD, 2000

KIDS

BASEBALL'S AN AGELESS GAME. BEFORE YOU KNOW IT, YOUNG STARS BECOME VETERAN HEROES, AND ALL THE WHILE ANOTHER YOUTH MOVEMENT IS THERE TO REPLENISH THE GAME.

DEREK JETER, 1998

MICKEY MANTLE, 1951

TED WILLIAMS, 1939

NOMAR GARCIAPARRA, 1998

ALBERT PUJOLS, 2001

STAN MUSIAL, 1942

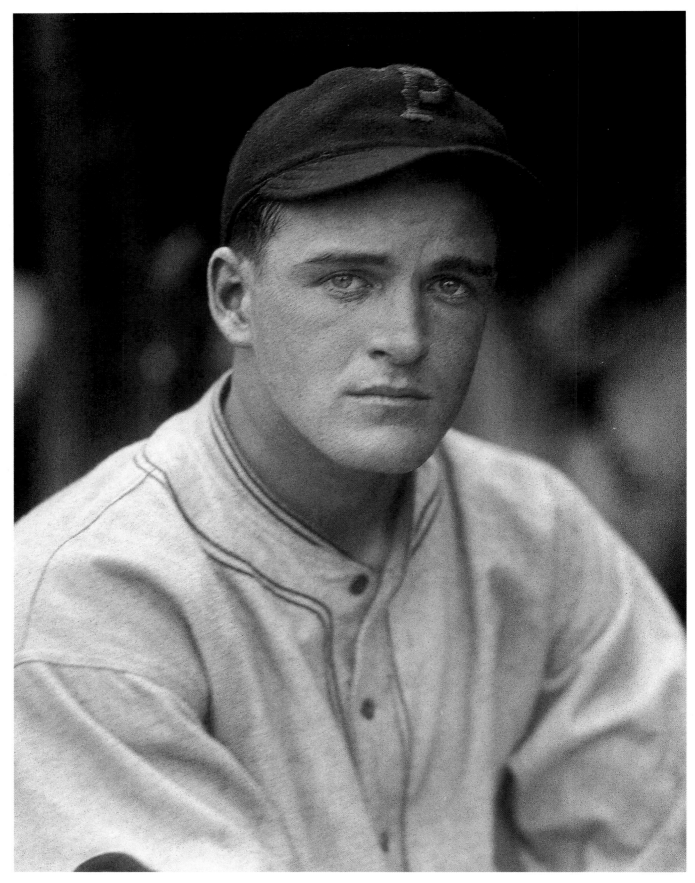

JOE CRONIN, 1926

Alex Rodriguez, 1996

PAT BURRELL, 1999

HARMON KILLEBREW, 1959

J.D. DREW, 1998

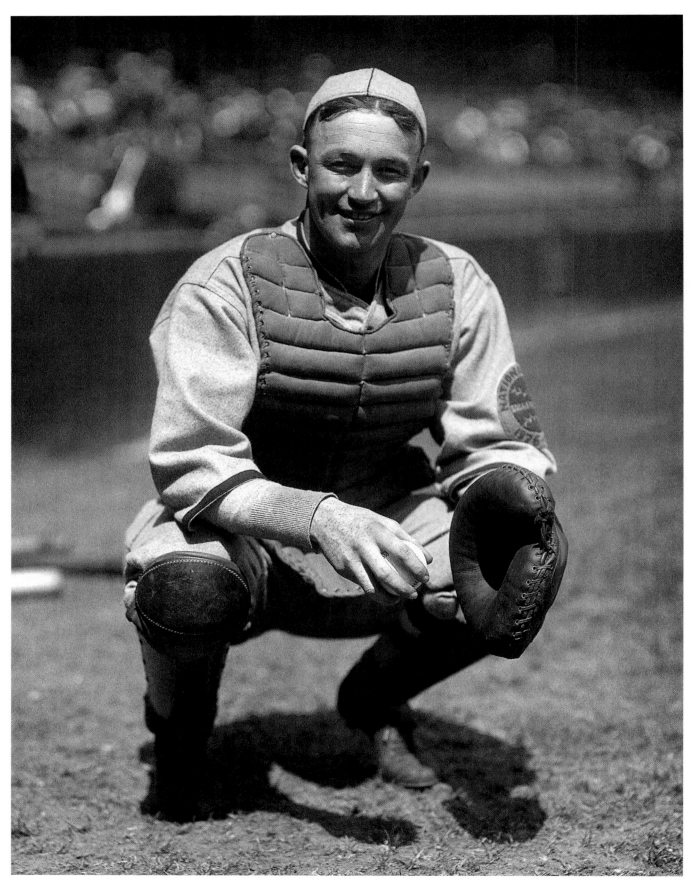

GABBY HARTNETT, 1925

JACKIE ROBINSON, 1944

BEN SHEETS, 2001

JIMMIE FOXX, 1926

LOU GEHRIG, 1925

RYAN ANDERSON, 2000

JUSTIN THOMPSON, 1996

HANK GREENBERG, 1933

JOE DiMAGGIO, 1936

JEFF CIRILLO, 1997

WARREN SPAHN, 1946

ZACK WHEAT & ZACK WHEAT JR., 1925

BRIAN JORDAN & BRYSON JORDAN, 1996

CHARLES JOHNSON, 2000

LEATHER

THEY BLOCK THE PLATE. THEY DIVE IN THE HOLE. THEY RACE INTO THE GAP AND THEY SCALE THE WALL. BASEBALL'S NOT JUST ABOUT SCORING RUNS. IT'S ABOUT GETTING 27 OUTS A GAME.

LOU BOUDREAU, 1939

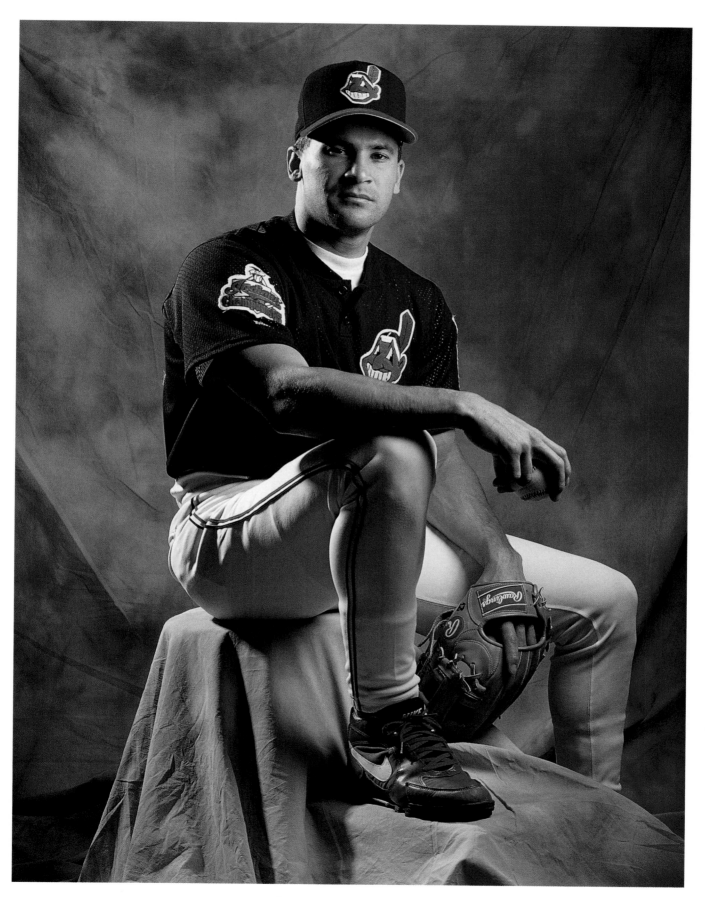

OMAR VIZQUEL, 1996

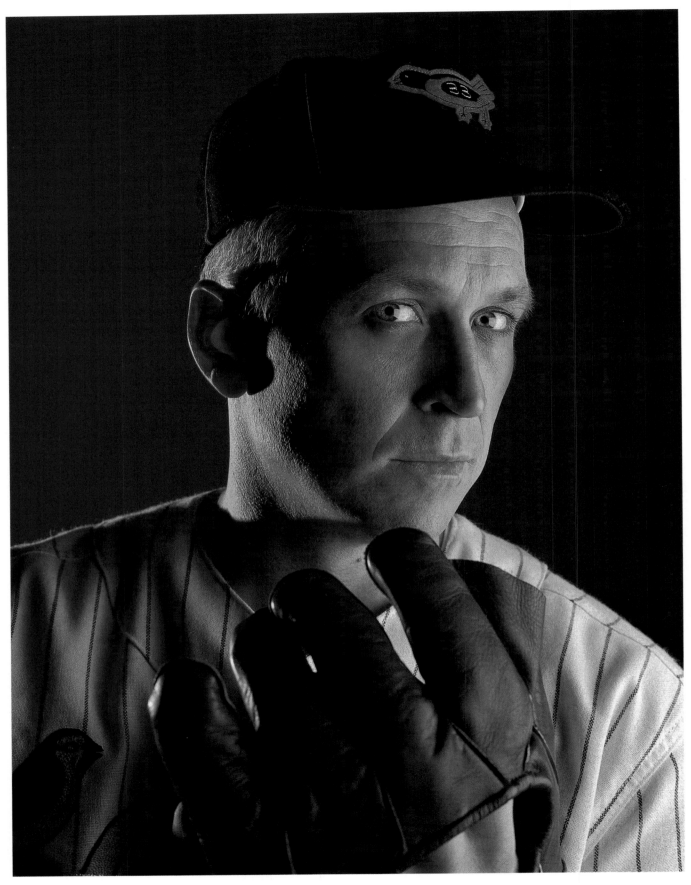

CAL RIPKEN JR., 1999

HONUS WAGNER, 1914

JOE CRONIN, 1932

CRAIG BIGGIO, 2001

JIM EDMONDS, 2000

MICKEY MANTLE, 1952

Tris Speaker, date unknown

Eric Davis, 1999

OZZIE SMITH, 1996

OZZIE SMITH, 1996

GEORGE SISLER, 1929

MATT WILLIAMS, 2000

CHARLIE O'BRIEN, 2000

BENNY BENGOUGH, 1932

Dom DiMaggio, 1940

BRIAN JOHNSON, 2000

ROBIN YOUNT, 1992

BERNIE WILLIAMS, 1993

Ivan Rodriguez, 2000

Ivan Rodriguez, 1997

HANK AARON, 1967

BARRY BONDS, 1999

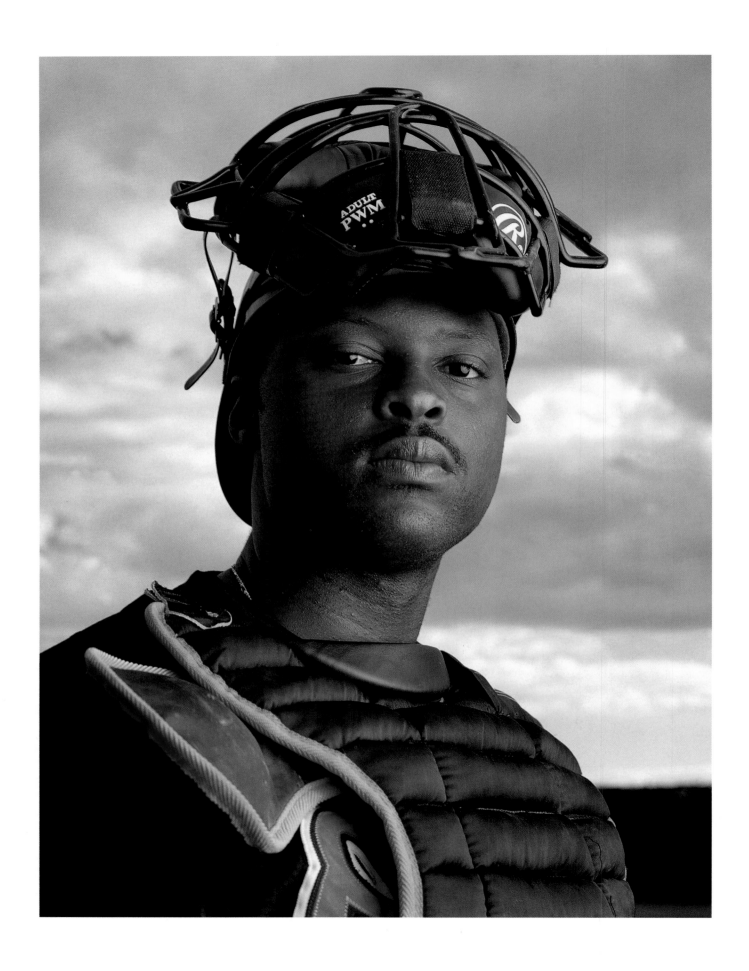

CHARLES JOHNSON, 2000

CLEVELAND INDIANS, 1995

(CLOCKWISE FROM TOP LEFT) TONY PEÑA, ALVARO ESPINOZA, JULIAN TAVAREZ, JOSE MESA, DENNIS
MARTINEZ, SANDY ALOMAR JR., JULIO FRANCO, CARLOS BAERGA AND MANNY RAMIREZ

Teammates

The '79 Pirates were Fam-i-lee. Jose and Big Mac were Bash Brothers. In the course of a 162-game season, players become more than just a bunch of guys in a locker room. They become teammates.

JAY BUHNER, ALEX RODRIGUEZ & KEN GRIFFEY JR., 1997

YOGI BERRA & JOE DiMAGGIO, 1950

RED SCHOENDIENST & STAN MUSIAL, 1963

CRAIG BIGGIO & JEFF BAGWELL, 1999

MARK MCGWIRE & JOSE CANSECO, 1997

MONTE IRVIN & WILLIE MAYS, 1951

EDDIE MATHEWS & HANK AARON, 1959

RON GANT, RAY LANKFORD & BRIAN JORDAN, 1996

HANK GREENBERG & CHARLIE GEHRINGER, 1934

Don Drysdale & Sandy Koufax, 1964

ROGER CLEMENS & PAT HENTGEN, 1997

BARRY BONDS & WILL CLARK, 1993

Carl Yastrzemski, Reggie Smith & Tony Conigliaro, 1970

TIM HUDSON, MARK MULDER & BARRY ZITO, 2001

TONY GWYNN, 1999

NATURALS

THEIR SWINGS ARE SWEET. THEIR HANDS
ARE SOFT. THEIR MOVEMENT IS SMOOTH.
THOUGH THEIR ABILITY HAS BEEN HONED
BY HOURS OF REPETITION, THE GAME
JUST COMES NATURALLY FOR SOME
MORE THAN OTHERS.

TY COBB, 1927

Nap Lajoie, 1915

DEREK JETER, 1999

DEREK JETER, 1997

Joe DiMaggio, 1938

MICKEY MANTLE, 1959

ICHIRO SUZUKI, 2001

ROBERTO CLEMENTE, 1958

VLADIMIR GUERRERO, 2001

ROGERS HORNSBY, 1929

ROGERS HORNSBY, 1925

KEN GRIFFEY JR., 1998

CAL RIPKEN JR., 2000

MICKEY COCHRANE, 1934

CHARLIE GEHRINGER, 1937

CRAIG BIGGIO, 2001

BILL DICKEY, 1929

ERNIE BANKS, 1964

ALEX RODRIGUEZ, 2000

JOE JACKSON, 1913

EDDIE COLLINS, 1925

TONY GWYNN, 1999

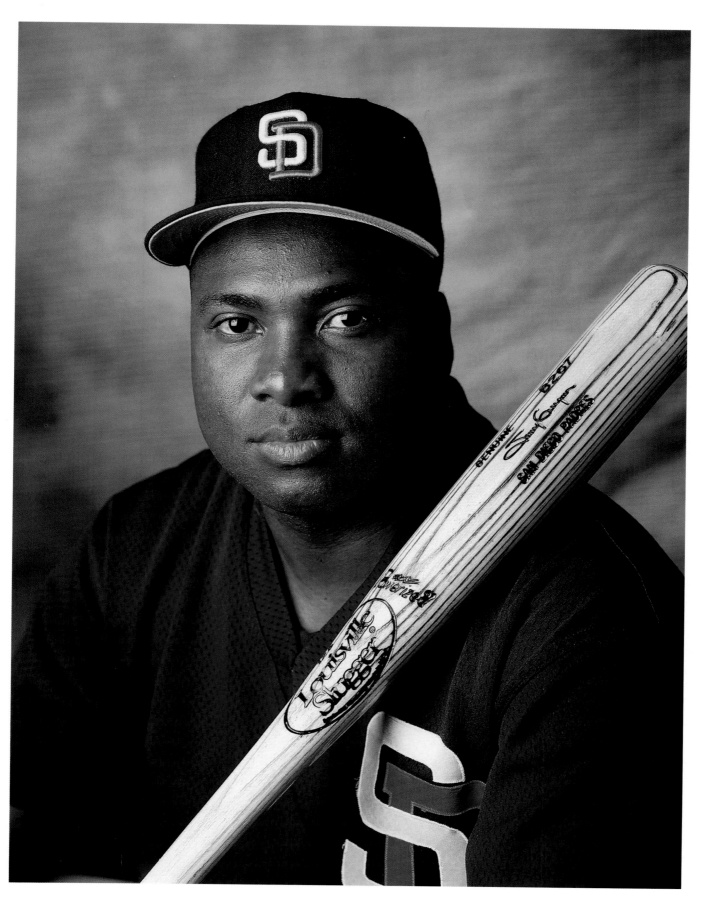

TONY GWYNN, 1997

LLOYD WANER, 1929

PAUL WANER, 1927

ROGER CLEMENS, 1999

ACES

Some take the ball every fifth day or so, entrusted to halt losing streaks and to win the big game. Some are out there every night, entrusted with one, two or three batters and to close out victories. Some are pure flame-throwers; some rely on cunning and guile more than sheer heat. There's a reason they're called aces.

ROGER CLEMENS, 1999

WALTER JOHNSON, 1914

MARIANO RIVERA, 2000

DIZZY DEAN, 1935

WHITEY FORD, 1957

118

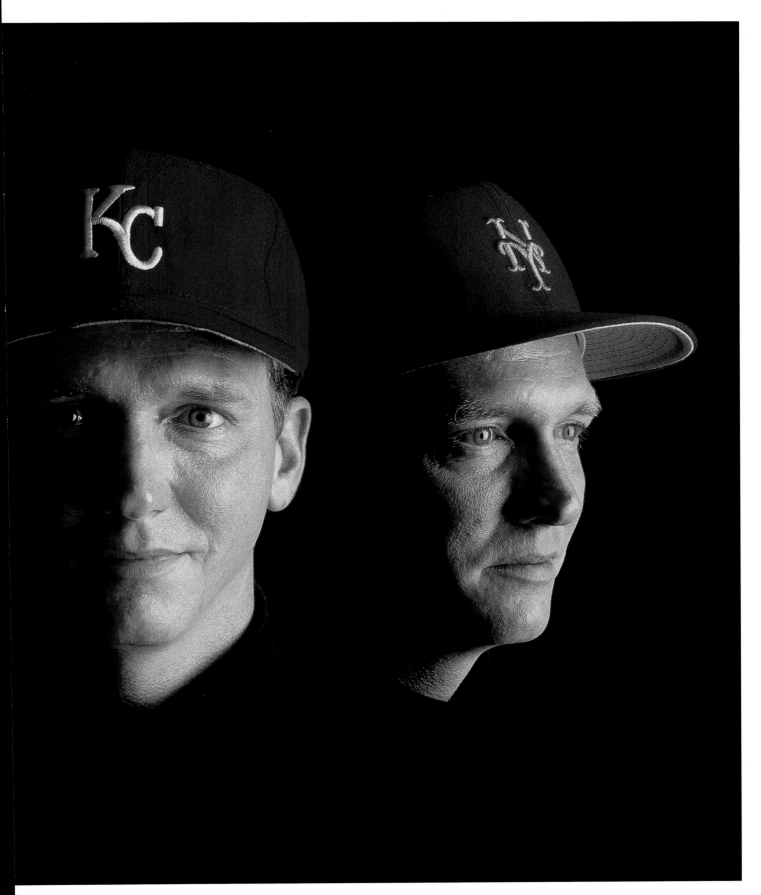

DAVID CONE, 1996

JOHN WETTELAND, 1997

GROVER CLEVELAND ALEXANDER, 1916

HERB PENNOCK, 1928

Pedro Martinez, 1998

ROBB NENN, 2001

Schoolboy Rowe, 1933

ANDY PETTITTE, 1996

DAVID WELLS, 2001

BOB FELLER, DATE UNKNOWN

PEDRO MARTINEZ, 2000

Mike Mussina, 1996

CHRISTY MATHEWSON, DATE UNKNOWN

JOHN SMOLTZ, 1999

RANDY JOHNSON, 1996

TOM GLAVINE, 2000

FRANK THOMAS, 1996

SLUGGERS

The Babe. Hammerin' Hank. Reggie.

Big Mac. Slammin' Sammy.

Home run hitters are

hard to forget.

HACK WILSON, 1926

JOHNNY MIZE, 1940

JUAN GONZALEZ, 2000

ANDRES GALARRAGA, 1998

BABE RUTH, 1927

HANK AARON, 1968

MARK McGWIRE, 1997

BARRY BONDS, 1997

HARMON KILLEBREW, 1964

HANK GREENBERG, 1945

MO VAUGHN, 1996

Hank Aaron, 1999

CHUCK KLEIN, 1936

JEFF BAGWELL, 1996

KEN CAMINITI, 1996

STEVE FINLEY, 1996

HARMON KILLEBREW, 1962

MARK McGWIRE, 1997

MIKE PIAZZA, 1998

MIKE PIAZZA, 1996

MEL OTT, 1933

MATT WILLIAMS, 1997

FRANK THOMAS, 2000

BARRY BONDS, 1999

EDDIE MATHEWS, 1965

CHIPPER JONES, 1998

JUAN GONZALEZ, 1997

DAVE WINFIELD, 1993

JIMMIE FOXX, DATE UNKNOWN

JOSE CANSECO, 1997

CECIL FIELDER, 1992

JOE CARTER, 1994

GABBY HARTNETT, 1932

FRANK THOMAS, 2000

CAL RIPKEN JR., 2000

LOU GEHRIG, 1927

LARRY WALKER, 1997

ANDRES GALARRAGA, 1996

SAMMY SOSA & MARK MCGWIRE, 1998

Tom Lasorda, 1996

Skippers & The Boss

Though the game is played between the white lines, so much of the game happens beyond, in the dugout, on the bench and even in the corporate offices.

JOHN McGRAW, DATE UNKNOWN

BOBBY VALENTINE, 1999

SPARKY ANDERSON, 1995

CASEY STENGEL, 1938

FELIPE ALOU, 1993

LEO DUROCHER, 1937

LEO DUROCHER, 1933

JIM LEYLAND, 1997

JOE TORRE, 1996

TOM LASORDA, 1996

JOE McCARTHY, 1935

MILLER HUGGINS, 1927

GEORGE STEINBRENNER, 1998

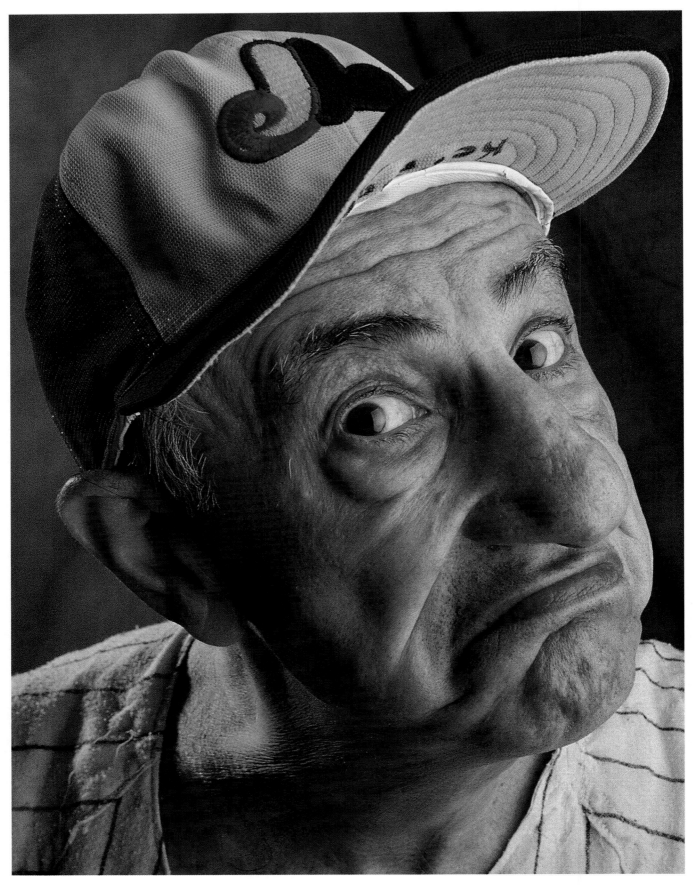

MAX PATKIN, 1996

Extra Innings

Baseball is a timeless game. There's no
clock, no time limit. Even after
nine innings the game can go on;
for some, the game goes on
for a lifetime.

VERDELL MATHIS, 1997

"THERE WERE 100 BETTER PLAYERS IN THE NEGRO LEAGUES THAN JACKIE (ROBINSON).
BUT WE WERE GLAD AS HELL BECAUSE IF JACKIE MADE IT, THEN WE COULD MAKE IT."

"I NEVER WANTED TO PLAY IN THE MAJOR LEAGUES. ALL I WANTED TO DO WAS TRAVEL. I JUST WANTED TO SEE FOUR PLACES IN THE COUNTRY BEFORE I DIED: NEW YORK, CHICAGO, CALIFORNIA AND NEW ORLEANS. I DID THAT. I CAN'T COMPLAIN ABOUT NOTHING."

CLIFFORD "CONNIE" JOHNSON JR., 1997

TED "DOUBLE DUTY" RADCLIFFE, 1997

"I USED TO LOVE TO GO TO HAVANA, CUBA, TO PLAY. YOU'D BE TREATED LIKE A MAN. THE WOMEN DOWN THERE USED TO LOVE ME. I DON'T KNOW HOW I PITCHED SOMETIMES."

"THE MONARCHS NEVER GOT GAS WHERE WE COULDN'T USE THE RESTROOM. WE NEVER PLAYED IN A TOWN WHERE THEY DIDN'T HAVE A PLACE FOR US TO STAY. JACKIE (ROBINSON) TAUGHT US THAT."

JOHN "BUCK" O'NEIL, 1997

JOE B. SCOTT, 1997

"WHEN YOU KNOW THAT RACISM EXISTS, THEN YOU GO ALONG WITH IT
AND JUST PLAY FOR THE LOVE OF THE GAME."

LESTER LOCKETT, 1997

"The Negro leagues were hard. We had to ignore the racism.
We had our work to do."

BABE RUTH, 1938

Honus Wagner, 1936

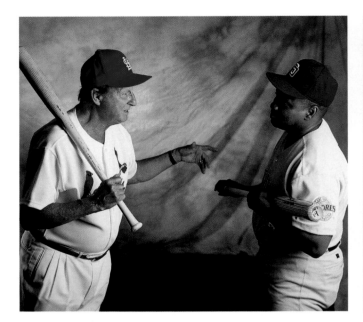

S<small>TAN</small> M<small>USIAL</small> & T<small>ONY</small> G<small>WYNN</small>, 1997

Bob Gibson, 1998

HANK AARON, 1999

GEORGE BRETT, 1993

OZZIE SMITH, 1996

Max Patkin, 1996

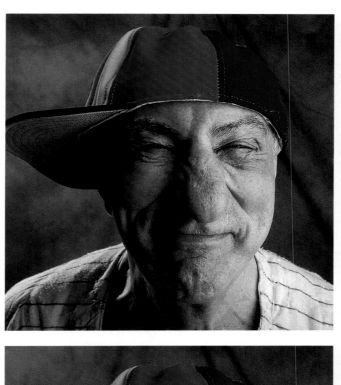

Photo Credits

Page 3—Robert Seale/The Sporting News. **Page 6**—(clockwise from top left) Robert Seale/The Sporting News; Charles Conlon/TSN Archives; Albert Dickson/The Sporting News; Charles Conlon/TSN Archives. **Page 8**—Albert Dickson/The Sporting News. **10**—Robert Seale/The Sporting News. **11**—TSN Archives. **12**—Charles Conlon/TSN Archives. **13**—Robert Seale/The Sporting News. **14**—Albert Dickson/The Sporting News. **15**—Charles Conlon/TSN Archives. **16**—Charles Conlon/TSN Archives. **17**—Robert Seale/The Sporting News. **18**—Robert Seale/The Sporting News. **19**—TSN Archives. **20-21**—Albert Dickson/The Sporting News. **22**—Charles Conlon/TSN Archives. **23**—TSN Archives. **24-25**—Albert Dickson/The Sporting News. **26, 27**—Charles Conlon/TSN Archives. **28**—Bob Leverone/The Sporting News. **29**—Robert Seale/The Sporting News. **30-31**—Charles Conlon/TSN Archives. **32**—Robert Seale/The Sporting News. **33**—TSN Archives. **34**—Charles Conlon/TSN Archives. **35**—Albert Dickson/The Sporting News. **36**—Robert Seale/The Sporting News. **38**—TSN Archives. **39**—Albert Dickson/The Sporting News. **40**—Robert Seale/The Sporting News. **41-42**—Charles Conlon/TSN Archives. **43**—Robert Seale/The Sporting News. **44**—Albert Dickson/The Sporting News. **45**—TSN Archives. **46**—Charles Conlon/TSN Archives. **47**—Robert Seale/The Sporting News. **48, 49**—TSN Archives. **50**—Charles Conlon/TSN Archives. **51**—Albert Dickson/The Sporting News. **52**—Robert Seale/The Sporting News. **53, 54**—Charles Conlon/TSN Archives. **55**—Robert Seale/The Sporting News. **56-57**—TSN Archives. **58-59**—Robert Seale/The Sporting News. **60**—TSN Archives. **61, 62, 63**—Robert Seale/The Sporting News. **64**—Albert Dickson/The Sporting News. **66**—Albert Dickson/The Sporting News. **67, 68**—TSN Archives. **69**—Robert Seale/The Sporting News. **70-71**—Albert Dickson/The Sporting News. **72, 73**—TSN Archives. **74**—Albert Dickson/The Sporting News. **75, 76**—TSN Archives. **77**—Robert Seale/The Sporting News. **78-79, 80**—TSN Archives. **81**—Albert Dickson/The Sporting News. **82**—Robert Seale/The Sporting News. **84, 85**—TSN Archives. **86, 87**—Robert Seale/The Sporting News. **88, 89**—TSN Archives. **90, 91**—Albert Dickson/The Sporting News. **92**—TSN Archives. **93**—Albert Dickson/The Sporting News. **94, 95**—Charles Conlon/TSN Archives. **96**—Albert Dickson/The Sporting News. **97**—Robert Seale/The Sporting News. **98, 99**—Charles Conlon/TSN Archives. **100**—Robert Seale/The Sporting News. **101**—Charles Conlon/TSN Archives. **102**—TSN Archives. **103**—Albert Dickson/The Sporting News. **104, 105**—Charles Conlon/TSN Archives. **106**—Robert Seale/The Sporting News. **107**—Albert Dickson/The Sporting News. **108, 109**—Charles Conlon/TSN Archives. **110-112**—Robert Seale/The Sporting News. **113**—Charles Conlon/TSN Archives. **114-115**—Robert Seale/The Sporting News. **116**—Charles Conlon/TSN Archives. **117**—TSN Archives. **118-119,120**—Albert Dickson/The Sporting News. **121-122**—Charles Conlon/TSN Archives. **123**—Robert Seale/The Sporting News. **124**—Albert Dickson/The Sporting News. **125**—Charles Conlon/TSN Archives. **126-127, 128, 129**—Albert Dickson/The Sporting News. **130**—Charles Conlon/TSN Archives. **131**—Robert Seale/The Sporting News. **132**—TSN Archives. **133**—Charles Conlon/TSN Archives. **134**—Robert Seale/The Sporting News. **135**—Albert Dickson/The Sporting News. **136-137**—Robert Seale/The Sporting News. **138**—Robert Seale/The Sporting News. **140, 141**—Charles Conlon/TSN Archives. **142, 143**—Robert Seale/The Sporting News. **144**—Charles Conlon/TSN Archives. **145**—TSN Archives. **146, 147**—Albert Dickson/The Sporting News. **148**—TSN Archives. **149**—Charles Conlon/TSN Archives. **150, 151**—Robert Seale/The Sporting News. **152**—Charles Conlon/TSN Archives. **153**—Robert Seale/The Sporting News. **154**—Robert Seale/The Sporting News. **155**—Albert Dickson/The Sporting News. **156**—TSN Archives. **157**—Albert Dickson/The Sporting News. **158, 159**—Robert Seale/The Sporting News. **160**—TSN Archives. **161**—Robert Seale/The Sporting News. **162**—Albert Dickson/The Sporting News. **163**—Robert Seale/The Sporting News. **164**—TSN Archives. **165**—Robert Seale/The Sporting News. **166, 167**—TSN Archives. **168**—Charles Conlon/TSN Archives. **169**—Albert Dickson/The Sporting News. **170, 171**—TSN Archives. **172**—Charles Conlon/TSN Archives. **173**—Albert Dickson/The Sporting News. **174**—Robert Seale/The Sporting News. **175**—Charles Conlon/TSN Archives. **176, 177**—Albert Dickson/The Sporting News. **178-179**—TSN Archives. **180**—Albert Dickson/The Sporting News. **182**—Charles Conlon/TSN Archives. **183**—TSN Archives. **184**—Albert Dickson/The Sporting News. **185**—Charles Conlon/TSN Archives. **186, 187**—TSN Archives. **188, 189**—Charles Conlon/TSN Archives. **190**—Robert Seale/The Sporting News. **191**—Albert Dickson/The Sporting News. **192, 193**—Albert Dickson/The Sporting News. **194, 195**—Charles Conlon/TSN Archives. **196, 197**—Albert Dickson/The Sporting News. **198**—Albert Dickson/The Sporting News. **200-211**—Albert Dickson/The Sporting News. **212, 213**—Charles Conlon/TSN Archives. **214, 215**—Albert Dickson/The Sporting News. **216**—Albert Dickson/The Sporting News. **217**—Robert Seale/The Sporting News. **218**—TSN Archives. **219**—Albert Dickson/The Sporting News. **220, 221**—Albert Dickson/The Sporting News.

PHOTO INDEX